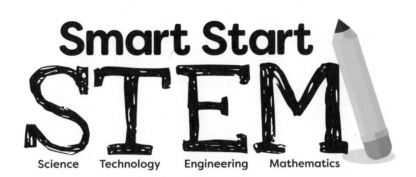

Smart Start STEM

Science   Technology   Engineering   Mathematics

1

Grade 1

Writing: Tiffany Rivera
Barbara Allman
Content Editing: Lisa Vitarisi Mathews
Copy Editing: Laurie Westrich
Art Direction: Yuki Meyer
Cover Design: Yuki Meyer
Illustration: Mary Rojas
Design/Production: Yuki Meyer
Jessica Onken

EMC 9927

Evan-Moor®
Helping Children Learn

Visit
teaching-standards.com
to view a correlation
of this book.
This is a free service.

**Correlated to
Current Standards**

EVAN-MOOR CORP.
phone 1-800-777-4362, fax 1-800-777-4332.
Entire contents © 2018 EVAN-MOOR CORP.
18 Lower Ragsdale Drive, Monterey, CA 93940-5746. Printed in China.

CPSIA: Asia Pacific Offset Ltd, Kowloon, Hong Kong [5/2019]

Contents

Physical Science

Concept: Solids, liquids, and gases are matter that have different properties.

Skills: Demonstrate understanding of what happens when a solid melts; Visual discrimination; Fine motor skills; Connect words and pictures; Letter formation; Demonstrate understanding of a mixture

STEM Challenge: Ice Cream Chunks

Concept: Liquids have physical properties.

Skills: Demonstrate understanding of liquid matter; Visual discrimination; Connect words and pictures; Word meaning; Letter formation; Sequencing; Inference

STEM Challenge: Keep It Dry

Concept: A system has parts that work together.

Skills: Match words to pictures; Visual discrimination; Letter formation; Demonstrate understanding of a system; Demonstrate understanding of the purpose of different systems; Make connections between sentences and pictures

STEM Challenge: Playground Systems

Concept: Sound is made when objects vibrate.

Skills: Comprehension; Letter formation; Sequencing; Inference; Match words to pictures; Fine motor skills

STEM Challenge: Music Sounds

Smart Start: STEM • EMC 9927 • © Evan-Moor Corp.

Life Science

Smart Start: STEM • EMC 9927 • © Evan-Moor Corp.

General Materials List

- aluminum can
- aluminum foil
- ball or other round object
- blankets
- bucket or tub
- buttons
- cardboard
- cardboard tubes
- cardstock or paper
- chairs
- clothespins
- coffee stirs
- cotton balls
- craft sticks
- egg cartons
- empty yogurt tins
- fabric
- feathers
- glue
- graham crackers
- grass
- gumdrops
- hardboiled egg
- icing
- marbles
- newspaper
- notecards
- packing peanuts
- paper
- paper clips
- paper cups
- paper towel rolls
- pencil

- pennies (30)
- pillows
- pipe cleaners
- plastic jar
- plastic wrap
- plate
- playdough or clay
- popsicle sticks
- rocks
- rubber bands
- ruler
- scissors
- sheets
- shoe box
- small soft ball
- sofa cushions
- spoons
- stopwatch or clock
- straws
- string
- strips of paper
- styrofoam
- styrofoam cups
- table
- tape
- tissue box
- toothpicks
- towel or paper towel
- twigs or sticks
- twist ties
- unsharpened pencils
- water
- wax paper

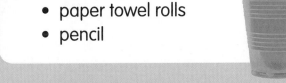

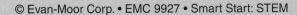

How to Use This Book

STEM: Science, Technology, Engineering, and Math

The STEM activities and challenges in this book are designed to be fun! Children are invited to think creatively and explore different ideas to solve problems. They engage in questioning, problem solving, collaboration, and hands-on projects. Parents act as facilitators, guiding their children through the problem-solving process and providing encouragement. The lessons in this book will help children understand science concepts and provide a foundation for completing the STEM challenges. Children who have opportunities to do STEM challenges learn to think critically and develop skills to become problem solvers who can find solutions to real-world problems.

Science Texts and Stories

Read the science text and the science story to your child, or if your child is able, have him or her read the science text to you. Discuss how the illustrations or photos help your child better understand the science concept. Help your child make connections between the science concept in the story and his or her own life.

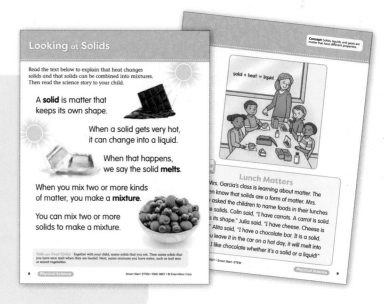

Activities

The written activities practice science concepts as well as basic skills such as writing, matching, and sequencing. Provide your child with support by reading the directions and answering any questions he or she may have.

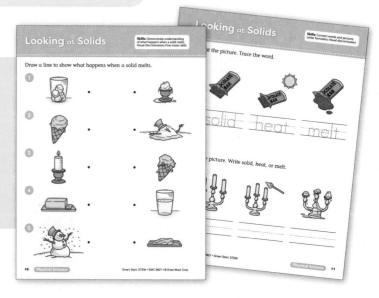

Smart Start: STEM • EMC 9927 • © Evan-Moor Corp.

STEM Stories

Read the STEM story to your child, or if your child is able, have him or her read the STEM story to you. Discuss the illustration and the problem in the story. Ask your child to share his or her ideas about how to solve the problem.

STEM Challenges

Use the information in the STEM Challenge to help you facilitate your child's experience.

- Read the Objective(s), the Challenge, and the Suggested Materials list. Then set up a place for your child to work. Feel free to add any materials you feel are appropriate for the challenge.

- Explain the Objective(s) and the Challenge to your child. Then guide your child through the steps of the STEM Process. It is important to note that there is not a "right" answer to a STEM Challenge. Children should be encouraged to explore their ideas and their creativity.

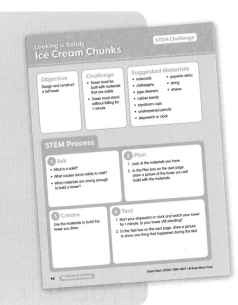

STEM Journals

The STEM Journal is based on the engineering design process. Provide support by reading the labels and any other text to your child. Explain to your child in simple terms that planning, creating, testing, and recording are all part of completing a STEM Challenge.

Looking at Solids

Read the text below to explain that heat changes solids and that solids can be combined into mixtures. Then read the science story to your child.

A **solid** is matter that keeps its own shape.

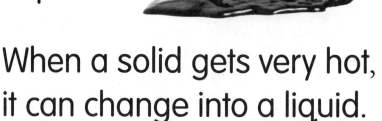

When a solid gets very hot, it can change into a liquid.

When that happens, we say the solid **melts**.

When you mix two or more kinds of matter, you make a **mixture**.

You can mix two or more solids to make a mixture.

Look at the picture and read the story.

STEM

There once was a king who lived in a castle made of windows. The king had a problem. The sun would shine through the windows and melt all of his favorite foods. His cheese melted, his ice cream melted, and his chocolate melted! He wanted his favorite foods to stay solid! Can you build the king a tall tower that does not have windows so he can go there to eat all of his favorite foods?

Looking at Solids
Ice Cream Chunks

Objective

Design and construct a tall tower.

Challenge

- Tower must be built with materials that are solids
- Tower must stand without falling for 1 minute

Suggested Materials

- notecards
- clothespins
- pipe cleaners
- rubber bands
- styrofoam cups
- unsharpened pencils
- stopwatch or clock
- popsicle sticks
- string
- straws

STEM Process

1 Ask

- What is a solid?
- What causes some solids to melt?
- What materials are strong enough to build a tower?

2 Plan

1. Look at the materials you have.
2. In the Plan box on the next page, draw a picture of the tower you will build with the materials.

3 Create

Use the materials to build the tower you drew.

4 Test

1. Start your stopwatch or clock and watch your tower for 1 minute. Is your tower still standing?
2. In the Test box on the next page, draw a picture to show one thing that happened during the test.

Smart Start: STEM • EMC 9927 • © Evan-Moor Corp.

Plan

Create: Use materials to build your project.

Test

Did it work? ☐ yes ☐ no

Looking at Liquids

Read the text below to explain that liquid is a state of matter. Then read the science story to your child.

Water is a **liquid**. A liquid flows from one place to another.

A liquid has no shape of its own. It takes the shape of the container that holds it.

You can pour, spill, splash, or spray liquids. Liquids can drip and flow.

Science

Kitchen Liquids

Trent's dog Quigley was thirsty, so Trent poured water into Quigley's dish. The water took the shape of the dish, because water is a liquid. Then Trent washed his hands with liquid soap. The soap flowed into his hand from the pump. Next, Trent decided to pour himself a cup of lemonade, but the cup tipped over, and the lemonade spilled. The lemonade spread out and dripped onto the floor. Trent said, "Oh no!" But Quigley didn't mind a bit!

Answer the question.
Fill in the circle for **yes** or **no**.

1

Does liquid take the shape of its container?

● yes   ○ no

2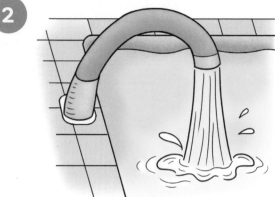

Is the water in the sink a liquid?

● yes   ○ no

3

Is soda in a can a liquid?

● yes   ○ no

4

Can a liquid spill out of its container?

● yes   ○ no

Look at the picture and read the story.

STEM

Zeke and his best friend Scarlett liked to play outside. One day it was so hot that after only one hour of playing, they felt tired and thirsty. They went inside the house, and Zeke filled two cups with water. As he handed one cup to Scarlett, both of the cups slipped from his hands and crashed onto the floor! Can you make two cups that are different shapes so the friends can drink water and tell which cup is theirs?

Objective

Design and construct two cups of different shapes that can hold water.

Challenge

- Construct two different cups that can hold at least ½ cup of water each
- Cups must be different shapes
- Water must not spill or leak out of cups for at least 1 minute

Suggested Materials

- water
- cardboard
- wax paper
- cardboard tubes
- towel or paper towel
- stopwatch or clock
- paper
- tape
- styrofoam

STEM Process

1 Ask

- What is a liquid?
- Does a liquid have a shape?

2 Plan

1. Look at the materials you have.
2. In the Plan box on the next page, draw a picture of the cups you will build with the materials.

3 Create

Use the materials to build the cups you drew.

4 Test

1. Place your cups on a paper towel.
2. Pour ½ cup of water into the cups you made.
3. Start the timer for 1 minute.
4. Watch your cups. Does water spill out the top? Does any water leak through the cups?
5. In the Test box on the next page, draw a picture to show one thing that happened during the test.

Plan

Create: Use materials to build your project.

Test

Did it work? ☐ yes ☐ no

Parts Work Together

Read the text below to introduce the idea that a system has parts that work together. Then read the science story to your child.

A **system** is made of parts that work together.

The **parts** of a system work **together** to do something that the parts cannot do by themselves.

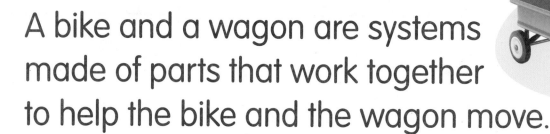

A bike and a wagon are systems made of parts that work together to help the bike and the wagon move.

A clock is a system made of parts that show the time.

All the parts in a system are important.

Talk with Your Child   Together with your child, look at the parts of the bike and the wagon. Ask your child to name the parts. Discuss what would happen if a part were missing. Then help your child find objects around the house that are simple systems and name their parts. Examples include a lamp, a camera, or a skateboard.

Smart Start: STEM • EMC 9927 • © Evan-Moor Corp.

Science

Tire Swing

Bernie is excited about the tire swing his dad built. His dad used a tire for the seat. Then he attached three strong chains to the tire. Next, he hooked those three chains to another chain. Last, he hung the tire swing to a big, thick tree branch. All of the parts of the tire swing are important; together, they form a system. The system would not work properly without one of the parts. Thank goodness Bernie's dad knows how a system for a tire swing works!

Parts Work Together

Skills: Match words to pictures; Visual discrimination; Letter formation

Draw a line to each part of the tire swing.
Then trace the words and read the sentence.

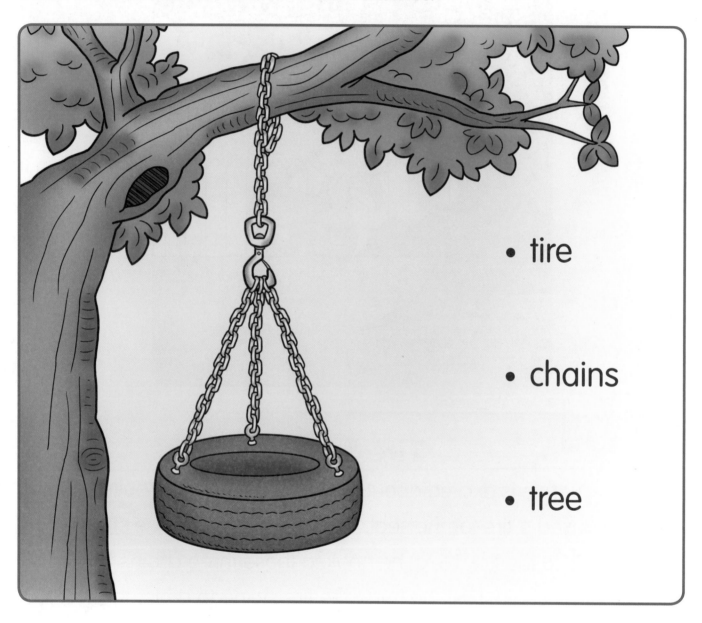

- tire

- chains

- tree

A _____swing_____ is a _____system_____.

Parts Work Together

Write a word to complete the sentence. Then read the sentence.

system   bike   parts

1 A ⬚⬚⬚⬚ is a system.

2 A ⬚⬚⬚⬚⬚ has parts.

3 The ⬚⬚⬚⬚⬚ work together.

Parts Work Together

Skills: Demonstrate understanding of the purpose of different systems; Make connections between sentences and pictures

Read the sentence. Look at the pictures.
Then draw a line to match the sentence to the system.

1 I can pull it. •

•

2 It heats a home. •

•

3 It tells time. •

•

4 It holds up my body. •

•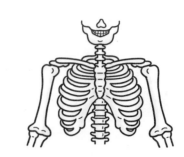

Look at the picture and read the story.

STEM

Charles likes to play with his friends at the park. He has a lot of fun sliding down the slide, swinging on the swings, and going up and down on the teeter-totter. But the playground is too far away from his home. Charles would like to have a playground in his neighborhood. Build one of the playground structures so Charles and his friends can play every day.

Objective

Design and construct a playground structure.

Challenge

- Structure must stand up
- Design must function as the actual play structure does (marble rolls down the slide, swings on swing, etc.)

Suggested Materials

- straws
- twist ties
- paper clips
- popsicle sticks
- unsharpened pencils
- rubber bands
- paper
- tape
- marble

STEM Process

1 Ask

- What is a system?
- What are some systems on a playground?
- What are the different parts needed for the playground system to work?

2 Plan

1. Look at the materials you have.
2. In the Plan box on the next page, draw a picture of the playground structure you will build with the materials.

3 Create

Use the materials to build the playground structure you drew.

4 Test

1. Stand your structure up. Does it stay standing?
2. Place the marble on your structure. Does the play structure work like a real one would?
3. In the Test box on the next page, draw a picture to show one thing that happened during the test.

Plan

Create: Use materials to build your project.

Test

Did it work? ☐ yes ☐ no

Making Sound

Read the text below to explain that sound is made when objects vibrate. Then read the science story to your child.

Sound is made when objects **vibrate**. When something vibrates, it is making a fast back-and-forth movement.

We can make musical instruments vibrate to make different sounds by banging a drum or plucking the strings of a guitar.

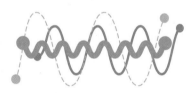

The sound you hear when an object vibrates is called a **sound wave**.

A sound wave travels through the air. Although you cannot see a sound wave, you can hear it!

Talk with **Your Child** Have your child look at the pictures above and name the instruments shown. Then have your child name instruments he or she has used or knows of. Together with your child, create sound waves by sitting at a table and using your hands to beat on the table like a drum.

Smart Start: STEM • EMC 9927 • © Evan-Moor Corp.

Science

The Sound Wave Dance

Sumiko wanted to learn about sound. She made a drum out of a coffee can and a balloon. She cut the balloon and stretched it over the top of the empty can. Then she put a rubber band around the can. Next, she poured sugar onto the balloon. Then Sumiko banged on a metal pan with a spoon. The sugar started to bounce around. Sound waves from the metal pan traveled through the air and made the balloon vibrate and the sugar move!

Making Sound

Skills: Comprehension; Letter formation; Sequencing

Circle the things that vibrate in the story.

Read the sentence. Trace the word or words.

1 The pan vibrates.

2 Sound waves travel.

3 I hear sound.

Making Sound

Read the word. Draw a line to the matching picture.

1 hit •   •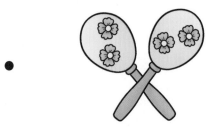

2 pluck •   •

3 blow •   •

4 shake •   •

Trace the word. Say the word out loud.
What instrument makes that sound? Draw a line to the picture.

1  •

•

2  •

•

3 twang •

•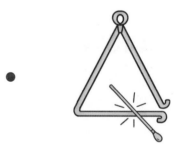

4 boom •

•

Look at the picture and read the story.

STEM

Gustavo hears a loud sound. He walks closer and closer to the sound to see where it is coming from. Gustavo turns the corner and sees his friend Marlin banging on a trash can. Marlin is making music—the trash can is his drum! "Do you want to make music with me?" asked Marlin. Gustavo would like to make music with him, but he doesn't have an instrument to play. Help Gustavo by making an instrument he can play.

Objective

Design and construct a musical instrument that makes two different sounds.

Challenge

Instrument must play two different sounds

Suggested Materials

- wax paper
- plastic wrap
- popsicle sticks
- rubber bands
- paper towel rolls
- aluminum can
- string
- tape
- plastic jar
- tissue box

STEM Process

1 Ask

- How is sound made?
- What are some ways to make sound?
- If you hit or blow on an instrument in different places, can it make more than one kind of sound?

2 Plan

1. Look at the materials you have.
2. In the Plan box on the next page, draw a picture of the instrument you will build with the materials.

3 Create

Use the materials to build the instrument you drew.

4 Test

1. Play your instrument. Can the instrument make two different sounds?
2. In the Test box on the next page, draw a picture to show one thing that happened during the test.

Smart Start: STEM • EMC 9927 • © Evan-Moor Corp.

Plan

↓

Create: Use materials to build your project.

↓

Test

Did it work? ☐ yes ☐ no

Read the text below to help your child learn the functions of the human brain and skull. Then read the science story to your child.

Every person has a **brain**. The brain is an important body part.

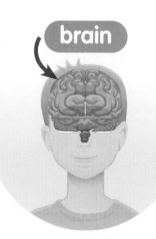
brain

The brain controls everything you do, from breathing and blinking to running and playing.

The brain is inside hard bones called the **skull**. The skull is in our head.

skull

It protects the soft brain from getting hurt.

Talk with Your Child Have your child look at the pictures and point to the brain and the skull. Ask your child to point to where the brain and skull are on his or her own body. Then discuss some ways you can protect your brain. For example, wearing a helmet when you ride your bike and wearing your seatbelt in the car.

 Smart Start: STEM • EMC 9927 • © Evan-Moor Corp.

Science

Use Your Brain

Noah's grandpa tapped him on the head. "Remember to use your brain today," he joked. Noah smiled. Of course he would use his brain! Noah knows that his brain is always working, even when he's asleep. Noah uses his brain to see, hear, touch, speak, and move. He uses it to learn and remember. Noah's brain is important. That's why it's inside his skull. The hard skull bones protect Noah's hardworking brain!

Skills: Demonstrate understanding of how a brain functions; Inference; Visual discrimination

Answer the question.
Fill in the circle for **yes** or **no**.

1

Does your brain still work when you are sleeping?

○ yes   ○ no

2

Is he using his brain to read?

○ yes   ○ no

3

Is he using his brain to run?

○ yes   ○ no

4

Can you see the boy's brain?

○ yes   ○ no

The **Brain** and **Skull**

Skills: Demonstrate understanding of body parts; Match words to pictures; Fine motor skills

Match the word with the picture.

1 brain •

2 skull •

3 protect •

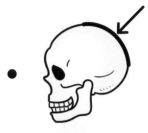

•

•

•

Finish the sentence to tell how your brain helps you.
Then draw a picture about the sentence.

My _____ helps me _____.

Life Science **43**

Skills: Demonstrate understanding of body parts; Match pictures to words; Visual discrimination

Label the picture. Write the words **brain** and **skull**.

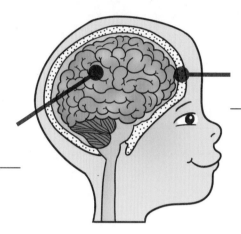

_____   _____

Draw an **X** on the pictures that show children protecting their brains.

Smart Start: STEM • EMC 9927 • © Evan-Moor Corp.

Look at the picture and read the story.

STEM

Humpty Dumpty loves to sit and play on the tall wall. He can see the entire town from the wall. But Humpty's mom worries that Humpty will fall down and hurt his brain. Help Humpty keep his brain safe by building something that will protect his head if he falls.

Life Science   **45**

Objective

Design and construct a device that will keep a hardboiled egg from breaking when it is dropped 3 feet.

Challenge

- Egg must be dropped from at least 3 feet high
- Egg must not break

Suggested Materials

- shoe box
- straws
- tape
- hardboiled egg
- packing peanuts
- rubber bands
- newspaper
- feathers
- cotton balls

STEM Process

1 Ask

- What protects the brain from being hurt?
- Why does an egg break when it is dropped?
- What materials will keep the egg from breaking?

2 Plan

1. Look at the materials you have.
2. In the Plan box on the next page, draw a picture of what you will build with the materials.

3 Create

Use the materials to build the device you drew.

4 Test

1. Put the egg in the device you built.
2. Drop the device from a height of 3 feet.
3. Did the egg crack or break?
4. In the Test box on the next page, draw a picture to show one thing that happened during the test.

The **Brain** and **Skull**
Humpty Dumpty

Plan

Create: Use materials to build your project.

Test

Did it work? ☐ yes ☐ no

Parts of an Insect

Read the text below to help your child learn about the parts of an insect. Then read the science story to your child.

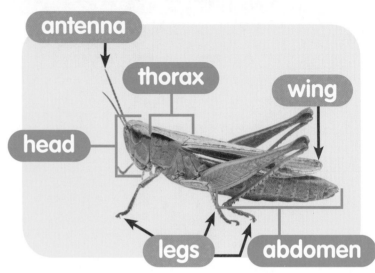

antenna
thorax
wing
head
legs
abdomen

A grasshopper is an **insect**. Insects have three main body parts.

The first part is the **head**. On the head, insects have eyes, a mouth, and two **antennae**.

The second part is the **thorax**. It is behind the head. The wings and the legs are attached to it. All insects have six **legs**. Only some insects have **wings**.

The third body part is the largest part of the grasshopper. It is the **abdomen**.

Talk with Your Child Look at the grasshopper diagram with your child. Have your child point to the different parts of the insect. Ask your child questions, such as: What body part has the legs and wings? How are the back legs different from the front legs? What is the biggest body part of an insect? Then go outside with your child and look for insects.

Smart Start: STEM • EMC 9927 • © Evan-Moor Corp.

Science

In the Grass

Lots of insects hide in grass. Today I held a grasshopper! See its head? It has two eyes, a mouth, and two antennae. The antennae help it feel and smell. Behind its head is the thorax. That is where the wings and legs are attached. Its back legs are for hopping. Its four shorter legs are for holding food and for walking. The rest of the grasshopper's body is called the abdomen. Now that I've looked at the grasshopper, it's time to set it free!

Skills: Demonstrate understanding of an insect's body parts; Visual discrimination; Matching words to pictures

Trace. Draw a line from the word to the correct part of the insect.

antenna

wing

•

•

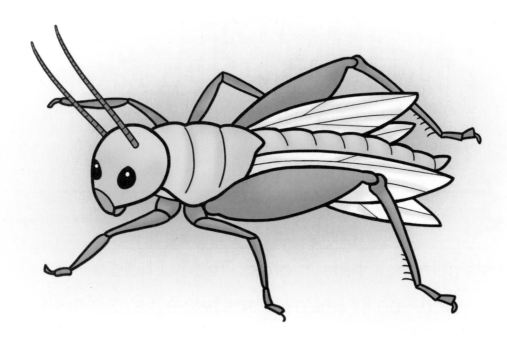

•

leg

Smart Start: STEM • EMC 9927 • © Evan-Moor Corp.

Parts of an Insect

Answer the question.
Fill in the circle for **yes** or **no**.

1

Does this butterfly have three main body parts?

◯ yes　　◯ no

2

Insects have six legs.
Is this spider an insect?

◯ yes　　◯ no

3

Ants do not have wings.
Is this ant an insect?

◯ yes　　◯ no

4

Is this bee an insect?

◯ yes　　◯ no

Parts of an Insect

Color only the insects.

Smart Start: STEM • EMC 9927 • © Evan-Moor Corp.

Look at the picture and read the story.

STEM

On Monday, Dalia saw a lot of butterflies. They flew up and down in the sky. On Tuesday, Dalia opened her window, but she did not see any butterflies. She went outside and looked for them, but she couldn't find them. She peeked into a beehive and discovered that the bees were gone, too! Insects are important to our world. Animals and plants need them. Help Dalia make a new insect to help our world.

Objective

Design and construct an insect.

Challenge

Insect must have head, thorax, abdomen, six legs, and two antennae

Suggested Materials

- playdough or clay
- toothpicks
- cardstock or paper
- pipe cleaners
- buttons

STEM Process

1 Ask

- What body parts does an insect have?
- Do all insects have wings?
- How many legs does an insect have?
- Do some insects have more body parts than other insects?

2 Plan

1. Look at the materials you have.
2. In the Plan box on the next page, draw a picture of the insect you will make with the materials.

3 Create

Use the materials to make the insect you drew.

4 Test

1. Look at your insect. Does it have all the body parts?
2. In the Test box on the next page, draw a picture to show one thing that happened during the test.

Smart Start: STEM • EMC 9927 • © Evan-Moor Corp.

Plan

↓

Create: Use materials to build your project.

↓

Test

Did it work? ☐ yes ☐ no

What Do Animals Eat?

Read the text below to explain that some animals are carnivores, some are herbivores, and some are omnivores. Then read the science story to your child.

Some animals eat meat. A meat eater is called a **carnivore**. Carnivores have sharp, pointed teeth.

Some animals eat plants. An animal that eats plants is called a **herbivore**. Herbivores have flat, wide teeth.

Other animals eat both meat and plants. They are called **omnivores**. Omnivores have sharp and flat teeth.

Talk with Your Child   Together with your child, talk about the food that each animal might eat. Talk about how the shape of animals' teeth may help them chew their food. Then ask your child how the shape of his or her teeth helps him or her eat.

Smart Start: STEM • EMC 9927 • © Evan-Moor Corp.

Animal Teeth

I have two pets. Pepper is a carnivore, or a meat eater. He uses his sharp, pointed teeth to bite and tear meat. Pepper gets excited when I give him a bone. Can you guess what Pepper is? He is my dog! My other pet is a pony named Pickles. She is a herbivore. She only eats plants. Her teeth are flat and wide for chewing and grinding hay. I have teeth like both of my pets, pointed and flat! That's because I'm an omnivore—I eat everything!

What Do Animals Eat?

Answer the question. Fill in the circle for **yes** or **no**.

Does a dog have sharp teeth?

○ yes   ○ no

Do a dog and a pony eat the same food?

○ yes   ○ no

Is this pony a herbivore?

○ yes   ○ no

Is this boy an omnivore?

○ yes   ○ no

Smart Start: STEM • EMC 9927 • © Evan-Moor Corp.

What Do Animals Eat?

Look at the pictures. Then circle the food the animal eats.

What Do Animals Eat?

Trace the word to complete the sentence.
Then read the sentence.

1  A cat eats meat.

2 A deer eats plants.

3  A wolf eats meat.

4  A cow eats plants.

Look at the picture and read the story.

STEM

Blair is walking through the woods with a basket of vegetables and meat when she hears a sound coming from the bushes. "I wonder what animal is making that sound," says Blair. Suddenly, an animal runs past her. "Oh my, I have never seen an animal like that! Come out, wild thing. I'll share my food with you," says Blair softly. Create the animal that Blair sees in the woods. Show its teeth so Blair knows what food to feed it.

Objective

Design and construct a new wild animal that is a carnivore, herbivore, or omnivore.

Challenge

- Animal must stand up on two or four legs for at least 20 seconds
- Animal's teeth must be shown
- Must be able to tell if the animal eats meat, plants, or both

Suggested Materials

- feathers
- paper cups
- cotton balls
- empty yogurt tins
- paper towel rolls
- glue
- paper

STEM Process

1 Ask

- What does a carnivore eat?
- What does a herbivore eat?
- What does an omnivore eat?
- What kind of teeth do meat eaters have?
- What kind of teeth do plant eaters have?

2 Plan

1. Look at the materials you have.
2. In the Plan box on the next page, draw a picture of the wild animal you will make with the materials.

3 Create

Use the materials to make the wild animal you drew.

4 Test

1. Put your animal in a standing position. Count to 20 seconds. Does it stay standing?
2. Look at your animal. Can you tell what the animal eats? Does it show its teeth?
3. In the Test box on the next page, draw a picture to show one thing that happened during the test.

Plan

Create: Use materials to build your project.

Test

Did it work? ☐ yes ☐ no

Where Animals Live

Read the text below to explain that a habitat is a place where animals live. Then read the science story to your child.

A **habitat** is a place where animals live, eat, and sleep.

A **forest** is one kind of habitat. It has many trees. Animals such as bears and foxes live in forests.

A **desert** is a habitat. It is very dry there. Snakes, lizards, and cactuses call it home.

An **ocean** is a habitat. Kelp, sharks, and fish live and grow in the ocean.

Talk with **Your Child**   Have your child look at the pictures above. Ask your child to point to each habitat. Discuss the weather in each habitat and the natural surroundings that provide safe shelter for the animals.

Smart Start: STEM • EMC 9927 • © Evan-Moor Corp.

Science

Animal Homes

Darla has a book about animals. She read about a bird called the elf owl. The elf owl lives in the desert. It rests in a hole in a cactus to protect itself from the hot sun and other animals. Then Darla read about a bird called a robin. It lives in the forest, high up in a tree. Squirrels and foxes live in trees, too. Last, she read about an octopus. It swims in the deep ocean. It hides in the kelp. Darla learned that different animals call different places home.

Where Animals Live

Skills: Comprehension; Inference; Letter formation

Read. Look at the pictures. Circle the correct answer.

1 Which animal lives in the desert?

2 Which plant gives an elf owl shelter in the desert?

3 What is the weather usually like during the day in the desert?

Trace the words. Then read the sentence.

A _desert_ is a _habitat_.

Where Animals Live

Draw a line from the word to the picture.
Then trace the words and read the sentence.

1 hole •

2 den •

3 nest •

4 A ‾forest‾ is a ‾habitat‾.

Where Animals Live

Follow the directions. Then color the picture.

① Draw 1

② Draw 2

③ Draw 3

④ Draw 4

Trace the words. Then read the sentence.

An ocean is a habitat.

Look at the picture and read the story.

STEM

Rona Robin loves living in the forest. There are many worms to eat. There are many trees to live in. There are many animals to be friends with. Rona loves the forest habitat so much, she plans to lay eggs there. But first, Rona needs to make a nest to keep her eggs safe and warm. Help Rona build a nest that will hold all of her eggs.

Objective

Design and construct a bird's nest.

Challenge

- Nest must be large enough to hold at least 3 eggs (marbles or rocks)
- Nest cannot be held together with glue
- Nest must stay intact with eggs inside when picked up

Suggested Materials

- twigs or sticks
- pipe cleaners
- strips of paper
- playdough
- 3 marbles or rocks
- grass

STEM Process

1 Ask

- What materials from nature do birds use to make their nests?
- Why does a bird need a nest?
- Where can you find a bird's nest?

2 Plan

1. Look at the materials you have.
2. In the Plan box on the next page, draw a picture of the bird nest you will make with the materials.

3 Create

Use the materials to make the nest you drew.

4 Test

1. Put eggs in the nest. Is the nest big enough to hold all the eggs?
2. Pick up your nest. Does it fall apart or stay together? Do the eggs stay inside the nest or fall out?
3. In the Test box on the next page, draw a picture to show one thing that happened during the test.

Smart Start: STEM • EMC 9927 • © Evan-Moor Corp.

Plan

Create: Use materials to build your project.

Test

Did it work? ☐ yes ☐ no

Animals in Winter

Read the text below to explain how animals survive during the winter. Then read the science story to your child.

The weather can be cold during the **winter**. Many animals have different ways to survive, or stay alive, during the winter.

Some animals like birds and butterflies survive by traveling to warmer places to find food. They **migrate**.

Other animals, like squirrels, stay where they are. They survive by collecting and storing food before winter comes.

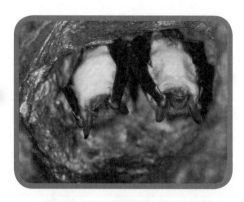

Animals like bears and bats **hibernate** during the winter. They sleep in a safe place until the weather gets warmer.

Talk with Your Child Have your child look at the pictures above and name the animals shown. Ask your child how people survive cold winter days (dressing warmly, staying inside the house, building a fire, etc.). Ask how animals' ways are different from or the same as people's ways.

Smart Start: STEM • EMC 9927 • © Evan-Moor Corp.

Science

Where Have the Animals Gone?

One winter day, Joey and Uncle Matt were walking home. "Where are all the animals?" asked Joey. "Some animals like bats and bears hibernate in the winter. That means they go into a deep sleep in a safe and warm place. Other animals like birds and butterflies migrate, or go where there is food and warmer weather. But animals like rabbits, mice, and squirrels stay in place. Animals survive winter in different ways," explained Uncle Matt.

Skills: Demonstrate understanding of how animals survive during winter; Visual discrimination

Answer the question. Fill in the circle for **yes** or **no**.

1

Does a squirrel migrate during winter?

○ yes   ○ no

2

Does a bear hibernate during winter?

○ yes   ○ no

3

Is the squirrel storing acorns in the ground to eat during winter?

○ yes   ○ no

4

Do squirrels and geese spend the winter in the same way?

○ yes   ○ no

   Smart Start: STEM • EMC 9927 • © Evan-Moor Corp.

Animals in Winter

Skills: Match words and pictures; Comprehension; Fine motor skills; Visual discrimination

Read the word. Circle the pictures that match the word.

 1  migrate

2 hibernate

3 stay in place

Animals **in** Winter

Skills: Demonstrate understanding of how animals survive during winter; Fine motor skills; Letter formation

Trace the words. Then draw a picture of an animal migrating and an animal hibernating. Color the picture.

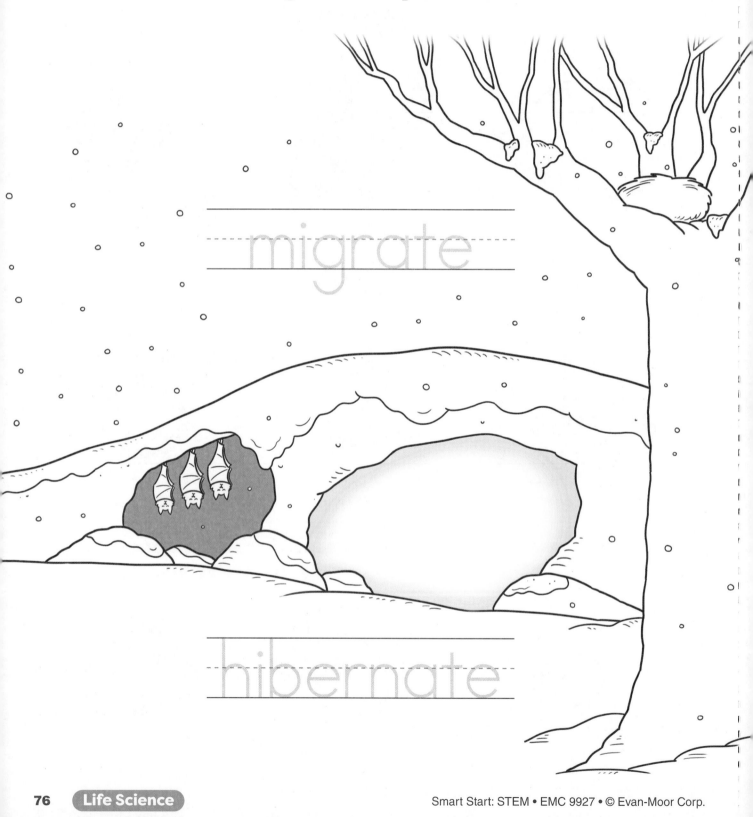

migrate

hibernate

Smart Start: STEM • EMC 9927 • © Evan-Moor Corp.

Look at the picture and read the story.

STEM

One cold winter night, Mom sat by the fireplace. "GRRR! I'm a little bear cub!" said her daughter, Gianna. "Hi there, little cub. Why are you in the house?" asked Mom. "I was cold outside, so I came in to sit by the fire," said Gianna. "Well, you should build your own cave, bear cub!" said Mom. "GRRR, that's a great idea," said Gianna. Can you help Gianna build a cave for a bear cub?

Bear Cave

Objective

Design and construct a cave.

Challenge

- Cave must be big enough to fit at least one "bear cub" (person)
- Cave must stand on its own for at least 15 seconds

Suggested Materials

- sofa cushions
- pillows
- blankets
- sheets
- table
- chairs

STEM Process

1 Ask

- What is a cave?
- Where are caves found?
- What animals live in a cave?
- What animals hibernate during the winter?
- How do animals keep warm in a cave during the winter?

2 Plan

1. Look at the materials you have.
2. In the Plan box on the next page, draw a picture of the cave you will build with the materials.

3 Create

Use the materials to build the cave you drew.

4 Test

1. Crawl into your cave. Do you fit inside? Can more than one "bear cub" fit inside?
2. Count 15 seconds. Does your cave stay standing?
3. In the Test box on the next page, draw a picture to show one thing that happened during the test.

Smart Start: STEM • EMC 9927 • © Evan-Moor Corp.

Plan

Create: Use materials to build your project.

Test

Did it work? ☐ yes ☐ no

Animals and Their Babies

Read the text below to explain that many baby animals look like their parents. Then read the science story to your child.

Many baby animals **resemble**, or look like, their parents. They have the same body parts, such as paws, and coverings, such as feathers.

Although they look like their parents, some baby animals have different names.

A baby bear is called a **cub**.

A baby goat is called a **kid**.

A baby cow is called a **calf**.

A baby deer is called a **fawn**.

A baby chicken is called a **chick**.

A baby pig is called a **piglet**.

Talk with Your Child Have your child point to and name the animals in the pictures above. Then ask your child if he or she knows any other animal babies that are named differently than their parents (a cat and a kitten, a dog and a puppy, a duck and a duckling).

Smart Start: STEM • EMC 9927 • © Evan-Moor Corp.

Science

Where's My Mama?

Yesterday, Lily played a game called "Where's My Mama?" First, Lily saw a big picture of a cub. Then she looked at small pictures of grown-up animals: a deer, a horse, and a bear. Which one is the mama? The bear's face, legs, paws, tail, and fur looked like the cub's. Lily clicked on the picture of the bear. Correct! A cub is a bear after it grows up. As Lily played the game she learned that baby animals usually look a lot like their parents!

Answer the question. Fill in the circle for **yes** or **no**.

1

Do they look like each other?

○ yes   ○ no

2

Is the cow the calf's mother?

○ yes   ○ no

3

Is the rabbit the duckling's mother?

○ yes   ○ no

4

Does the piglet look like the pig?

○ yes   ○ no

Smart Start: STEM • EMC 9927 • © Evan-Moor Corp.

Animals and Their Babies

Skills: Visual discrimination; Match pictures to words; Comprehension; Letter formation

Trace and read. Then draw a line to the correct picture.

1 cub •

2 calf •

3 fawn •

4 foal •

5 duckling •

Animals and Their Babies

Skills: Visual discrimination; Match pictures to words; Comprehension; Letter formation

Write the baby's name. Then circle the animal it becomes.

kid　　cub　　piglet　　chick

1

goat　　cow

2

pig　　chicken

3

bear　　rabbit

4

cow　　pig

Smart Start: STEM • EMC 9927 • © Evan-Moor Corp.

Look at the picture and read the story.

STEM

Farmer John has many animals that live on his farm. Mommy pig is one of them. Mommy Pig has 8 baby piglets. The piglets like to run all around the farm, and it is hard for Farmer John to find them. Help Farmer John build a square pigpen that will keep Mommy Pig and her 8 piglets safe.

Pigpen

Objective

Design and construct a square pigpen.

Challenge

- Pen must be in the shape of a square
- Pen must hold 9 "pigs"
- Pen must stand up on its own
- "Pigs" must fit in the pen without touching the sides of it

Suggested Materials

- tape
- paper clips
- 9 cotton balls
- toothpicks
- coffee stirs
- popsicle sticks
- playdough or clay

STEM Process

1 Ask

- What is a pigpen?
- How many sides does a square have?
- What is the size of a "pig"?
- Why do pigs need a pigpen?

2 Plan

1. Look at the materials you have.
2. In the Plan box on the next page, draw a picture of the pigpen you will build with the materials.

3 Create

Use the materials to build the pigpen you drew.

4 Test

1. Stand up your pigpen.
2. Place your 9 "pigs" in the pen. Do they all fit? Are the pigs touching the sides?
3. In the Test box on the next page, draw a picture to show one thing that happened during the test.

 Smart Start: STEM • EMC 9927 • © Evan-Moor Corp.

Plan

Create: Use materials to build your project.

Test

Did it work?   ☐ yes   ☐ no

The Moon

Read the text below to explain that the moon is a big ball of rock that moves around the Earth. Then read the science story to your child.

We can see the **moon** shining in the sky at night.

craters

The moon is a big ball of rock that moves around the Earth. There is no air on the moon, but there are mountains, flat lands, rocks, and big holes called **craters**.

The moon looks bright because the sun shines on it and lights it up. The moon seems to change shape, but that is because we can only see the part of it that is lit up by the sun. The shapes of the moon we see are called the **phases of the moon**.

moon phases

Talk with Your Child   Together with your child, look at the night sky. Have your child point to the moon and tell you what he or she knows about it.

Smart Start: STEM • EMC 9927 • © Evan-Moor Corp.

Science

Big Brother and the Big Moon

My big brother Neil reads books about the moon. He says the moon looks small, but it isn't. The moon is a big ball of rock that is very far away. Neil says it has big holes called craters. The moon looks like it changes shape, but Neil says it doesn't. The sun lights up the moon, so we only see the part that is lit. Neil says the moon has no air. That's why plants, animals, and people can't live on the moon. I'm going to look at the moon with Neil tonight!

The Moon

Skills: Demonstrate knowledge of the moon; Comprehension

Answer the question. Fill in the circle for **yes** or **no**.

Is the moon far from Earth?

○ yes   ○ no

Is the moon smooth?

○ yes   ○ no

Do trees and animals live and grow on the moon?

○ yes   ○ no

Does the moon change shape?

○ yes   ○ no

Write the words below to complete the sentences.
Then draw a picture of yourself on the moon.

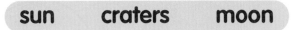

sun   craters   moon

1 The ☐☐☐☐ is a big ball of rock.

2 The moon has big holes called

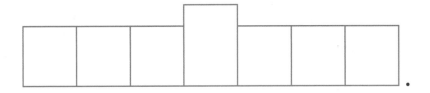

☐☐☐☐☐☐ .

3 Light from the ☐☐☐ makes
the moon shine bright.

The Moon

Look at the first picture. Draw an **X** on the picture that matches it.

1

full moon

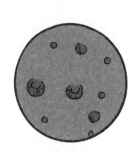 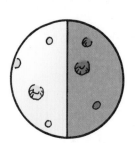 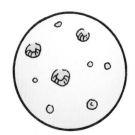

2

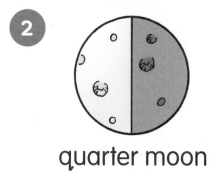
quarter moon

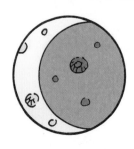 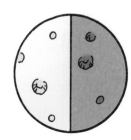 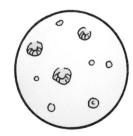

3

dark moon

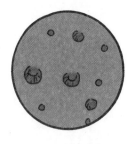 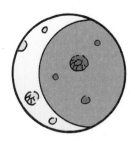 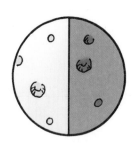

4

 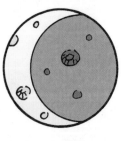
crescent moon

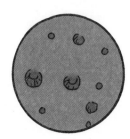 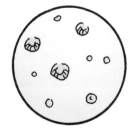 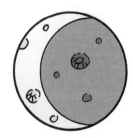

Smart Start: STEM • EMC 9927 • © Evan-Moor Corp.

Look at the picture and read the story.

STEM

  Hey Diddle, Diddle, did you say that a cow jumped over the moon? But how? My name is Tyson, and this is my dog, Diddle, Diddle. We want to jump over the moon, too, but we can't think of a way to do it. We can't fly. We can't jump that high. Can you build us something that will send us flying over the moon like that cow?

Objective

Design and construct a catapult or another device that will move one small object (a cow) over one large circular object (the moon).

Challenge

One small object must travel over one large circular object

Suggested Materials

- craft sticks
- spoons
- ruler
- rubber bands
- egg cartons
- paper towel rolls
- ball or other object for "moon"
- small soft ball for "small object"

STEM Process

1 Ask

- What can you do to make a small object move over a large object?
- How does your arm move when it throws something?
- How do your legs move when you jump?

2 Plan

1. Look at the materials you have.
2. In the Plan box on the next page, draw a picture of the device you will make with the materials.

3 Create

Use the materials to make the device you drew.

4 Test

1. Place your "cow" on the device.
2. Place your "moon" at least 6 inches from your device.
3. Send your "cow" flying over the "moon." Did the "cow" jump over the "moon"?
4. In the Test box on the next page, draw a picture to show one thing that happened during the test.

Plan

Create: Use materials to build your project.

Test

Did it work? ☐ yes ☐ no

Recording the Weather

Read the text below to help your child understand that changes in weather can be observed, described, measured, and recorded. Then read the science story to your child.

Weather changes from season to season and day to day. We use tools to measure weather.

One tool is a **thermometer**. It measures the temperature, or how hot or cold something is.

rain gauge

Another tool is called a **weather vane**, or **wind vane**. A weather vane shows which direction the wind is blowing: north, south, east, or west.

The next tool is called a **rain gauge**. It measures how much rain has fallen.

Talk with **Your Child**   Together with your child, name places where you have seen these weather tools being used. Maybe you have them on your home, or maybe one of your neighbors has them on his or her home. Maybe your child's school has a thermometer on the wall.

Science

Riley and the Weather

Riley is recording how the weather changes from day to day. She writes the temperature and weather symbols on her calendar every day. Today the thermometer says 80 degrees. The air feels warm and so does the wind. Riley looks up and sees the sun shining. She writes 80 degrees on the calendar. Then she draws the symbols for wind and sun on the calendar. "The weather is perfect today!" Riley exclaims.

Recording the Weather

Read the words. Look at the pictures.
Write the word to tell about the weather.

Monday	Tuesday	Wednesday	Thursday	Friday
windy	sunny	cloudy	rainy	snowy

1 Monday was _____.

2 Tuesday was _____.

3 Wednesday was _____.

4 Thursday was _____.

5 Friday was _____.

Smart Start: STEM • EMC 9927 • © Evan-Moor Corp.

Recording the Weather

Skills: Demonstrate understanding of weather symbols; Inference; Fine motor skills

Draw a weather symbol in the boxes to tell about the weather.

Recording the Weather

Skills: Demonstrate understanding of weather tools; Visual discrimination; Fine motor skills

What tool would you use to record the weather? Draw a line to match.

1

2

3

Look at the picture and read the story.

STEM

Hello! My name is Windy, and I am a flying squirrel. I fly from tree to tree and collect acorns. You see, I can't actually fly, but when the wind blows, I can open my arms and glide in the air. There are many trees that have acorns I want to eat, but I don't know which way the wind is blowing, so I'm not sure which tree I should glide to. Can you make me a tool that will tell me which direction the wind is blowing?

Strong Winds

Objective

Design and construct a tool that shows which direction the wind is blowing.

Challenge

- Tool must move to show which direction the wind is blowing
- Tool must stand on its own

Suggested Materials

- cup
- fabric
- glue
- gumdrops
- paper clips
- pencil
- popsicle stick
- paper
- straws

STEM Process

1 Ask

- What tools do you know about that show which direction the wind is blowing?
- What parts of your body can you use to find out which way the wind is blowing?

2 Plan

1. Look at the materials you have.
2. In the Plan box on the next page, draw a picture of the wind tool you will build with the materials.

3 Create

Use the materials to build the wind tool you drew.

4 Test

1. Stand your tool up. Does it stay standing?
2. Blow on your tool or leave it outside on a windy day. Does it move or spin? Can you tell how hard the wind is blowing by looking at your device?
3. In the Test box on the next page, draw a picture to show one thing that happened during the test.

Plan

Create: Use materials to build your project.

Test

Did it work? ☐ yes ☐ no

Bodies of Water

Read the text below to help your child identify and describe a variety of natural bodies of water. Then read the science story to your child.

Most of Earth's water is in **oceans**. An ocean is a large body of salt water.

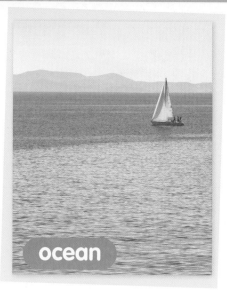
ocean

lake

Lakes are smaller bodies of water and are surrounded by land. Most have fresh water.

Rivers and **streams** also have fresh water. They are bodies of water that flow, or move in one direction. A river is wide, but a stream is narrow.

river

Talk with Your Child Discuss the differences between each body of water (ocean, lake, river, stream). Talk with your child about a body of water he or she has seen. Discuss the activities you can do at each body of water (sail a boat, swim, whale watching, etc.).

ocean

lake

river

stream

Science

Bodies of Water Everywhere

My family and I traveled around the world. That's how I found out that most of Earth is covered by water. It has oceans, lakes, rivers, and streams. I learned that oceans are the largest and deepest bodies of water. Then I found out that lakes are surrounded by land. My mom explained that rivers and streams are bodies of water that flow, or move in one direction. Boats can sail down rivers, but not streams. Streams are narrow and good for fishing!

Skills: Demonstrate understanding of different bodies of water; Visual discrimination; Comprehension

Answer the question. Fill in the circle for **yes** or **no**.

1

Is an ocean the largest body of water?

○ yes   ○ no

2

Does a lake have land all around it?

○ yes   ○ no

3

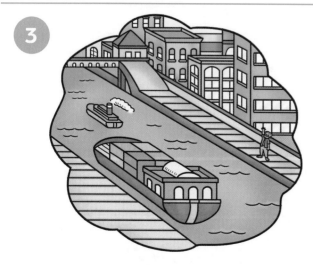

Does water in a river flow?

○ yes   ○ no

4

Is this stream bigger than a river?

○ yes   ○ no

Bodies of Water

Skills: Demonstrate understanding of different bodies of water; Visual discrimination; Comprehension; Match words to pictures

Look at the picture. Then trace the word that tells about the picture.

river   lake   stream   ocean

1

ocean

2

lake

3

river

4

stream

Bodies of Water

Read the question. Fill in the circle.

1 Which is the deepest?
- ○ ocean
- ○ river

2 Which has land all around it?
- ○ stream
- ○ lake

3 Which is more narrow?
- ○ stream
- ○ river

4 Which has large waves?
- ○ ocean
- ○ stream

Look at the picture and read the story.

STEM

Mr. Yoshida's class went on a field trip to see the baby birds in their nests. He told his class that last week during the heavy rains, three nests with babies had been spotted in the trees across from the stream. When Mr. Yoshida and his 30 students arrived they saw that part of the bridge had washed away. Now how would they be able to see the baby birds? Can you build a bridge to help Mr. Yoshida and his students cross the stream?

Bodies of Water
A New Bridge

Objective

Design and construct a bridge that will hold 30 students (pennies) over a plate of water.

Challenge

- Must only use three materials
- Bridge must stand on its own and be lifted off the ground by at least 2 inches
- Bridge must hold 30 pennies for 20 seconds

Suggested Materials

- straws
- scissors
- tape
- paper
- 30 pennies
- craft sticks
- cup
- water
- plate

STEM Process

1 Ask

- What does a bridge look like?
- What will help make a bridge strong?
- Does a cup full of 30 pennies feel light or heavy in your hands?

2 Plan

1. Look at the materials you have.
2. In the Plan box on the next page, draw a picture of the bridge you will build with the materials.

3 Create

Use the materials to build the bridge you drew.

4 Test

1. Stand your bridge up. Does it stay standing?
2. Place the bridge over a plate of water.
3. Place a cup of 30 pennies on the bridge.
4. Count 20 seconds. Does the bridge stay standing? Does the cup tip over and fall?
5. In the Test box on the next page, draw a picture to show one thing that happened during the test.

Plan

Create: Use materials to build your project.

Test

Did it work? ☐ yes ☐ no

Looking at Rocks

Read the text below to explain that rocks are changed by the weathering effects of wind, water, and ice. Then read the science story to your child.

Rocks are very hard, but they can be changed.

When natural forces such as wind, water, and ice change rocks, it's called **weathering**.

Wind, water, ice, and other forces cause rocks to fall, break, and become smooth. Big rocks become small rocks. Over many years, the small rocks get smaller and smoother until they become sand or soil.

Living things such as plants and animals can also break down rocks.

Talk with Your Child Together with your child, talk about the rocks near your home or in the area in which you live. Talk about how the rocks may have become the shape and size they are now.

Smart Start: STEM • EMC 9927 • © Evan-Moor Corp.

Science

Eric's Day at the Beach

Eric and his grandfather were walking on the beach. Eric's grandfather said, "These rocks used to be a part of that cliff." Eric watched the waves crash against the cliff. "One day," said his grandfather, "that piece of cliff will come crashing down. The rocks will break when they fall." Eric saw that the tiny grains of sand were the same color as the rocks. The sand had been part of that cliff, too!

Looking at Rocks

Skills: Demonstrate understanding of weathering; Visual discrimination

Answer the question. Fill in the circle for **yes** or **no**.

Can the wind change rocks by blowing them around?

○ yes　　　○ no

Can tree roots break up soil and rocks?

○ yes　　　○ no

Can ice break a rock apart?

○ yes　　　○ no

Can water change rocks over time?

○ yes　　　○ no

Smart Start: STEM • EMC 9927 • © Evan-Moor Corp.

Looking at Rocks

Skills: Match pictures to words; Sequencing; Visual discrimination

Draw a line to match the picture to the sentence.

1

The wave crashed against the cliff.

2

The rocks fell off the cliff.

3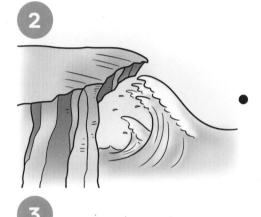

The rocks broke into small pieces.

4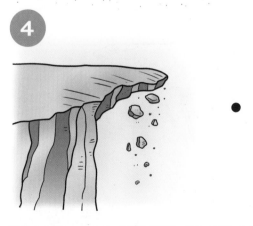

The rocks broke into even smaller pieces, then became sand.

Looking at Rocks

Read the sentence. Then draw a line to match the sentence to the picture.

1   Water wears away rocks.   •

•

2   Animals break rocks.   •

•

3   The wind blows rocks.   •

•

4   Ice breaks rocks apart.   •

•

Look at the picture and read the story.

STEM

Sabrina's house is built on a cliff. Sometimes the water hits the side of the cliff. Sometimes the wind blows very hard, knocking other rocks and sand on the cliff. Many plants and animals live by the cliff. The animals like to climb on top of the cliff and build tunnels below it. Sabrina wants to make sure her home stays standing for a long time. She needs your help. Build a device that will keep the waves from hitting the cliff.

Weathering Cliff

Objectives

- Design and construct a cliff.
- Design and construct a device that will protect the cliff from water.

Challenge

- Cliff must be at least 3 inches high and 3 inches wide
- Cliff must stand on its own

Suggested Materials

- aluminum foil
- cotton balls
- bucket or tub
- graham crackers
- playdough or clay
- popsicle sticks
- straws
- water
- icing

STEM Process

1 Ask

- What can change the size, shape, and texture of rocks?
- What materials will soak up water?

2 Plan

1. Look at the materials you have.
2. In the Plan box on the next page, draw a picture of the cliff and protection device you will build with the materials.

3 Create

Use the materials to build the cliff and protection device you drew.

4 Test

1. Stand your cliff up. Does it stay standing?
2. Place your cliff and your protection device in a tub. Fill the empty side of the tub with water.
3. Gently move the tub back and forth for 15 seconds. Does the water go through your protection device? Does the water hit the cliff?
4. In the Test box on the next page, draw a picture to show one thing that happened during the test.

Plan

Create: Use materials to build your project.

Test

Did it work? ☐ yes ☐ no

Smart Start
STEM
Certificate

_____

Name

Congratulations!

You planned, created,
and tested the things
you made!
You solved problems
and helped people!

Evan-Moor
Helping Children Learn

Answer Key

Samples of completed STEM challenges are pictured below. These are meant to serve as examples of possible outcomes of the challenges. The outcome of each challenge will vary depending on the child's approach and the materials used.

Looking at Solids

Page 10

Page 11
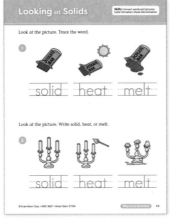

Page 12

Sample of a completed
Ice Cream Chunks
STEM Challenge

Looking at Liquids

Page 18

Page 19

Page 20
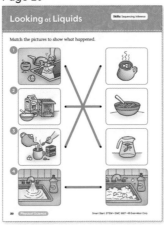

Sample of a completed
Keep It Dry STEM Challenge

Parts Work Together

Page 26

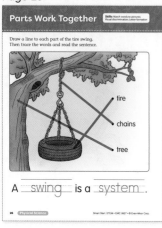

Parts Work Together

Draw a line to each part of the tire swing.
Then trace the words and read the sentence.

tire
chains
tree

A _swing_ is a _system_.

Page 27

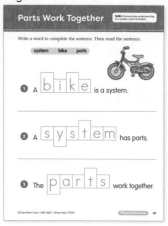

Parts Work Together

Write a word to complete the sentence. Then read the sentence.

system   bike   parts

1. A |b|i|k|e| is a system.

2. A |s|y|s|t|e|m| has parts.

3. The |p|a|r|t|s| work together.

Page 28

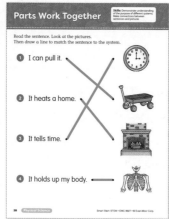

Parts Work Together

Read the sentence. Look at the pictures.
Then draw a line to match the sentence to the system.

1. I can pull it.
2. It heats a home.
3. It tells time.
4. It holds up my body.

Making Sound

Page 34

Making Sound

Circle the things that vibrate in the story.

Read the sentence. Trace the word or words.

1. The pan vibrates.
2. Sound waves travel.
3. I hear sound.

Page 35

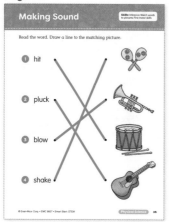

Making Sound

Read the word. Draw a line to the matching picture.

1. hit
2. pluck
3. blow
4. shake

Page 36

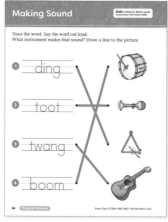

Making Sound

Trace the word. Say the word out loud.
What instrument makes that sound? Draw a line to the picture.

1. ding
2. toot
3. twang
4. boom

The Brain and Skull

Page 42

The Brain and Skull

Answer the question.
Fill in the circle for **yes** or **no**.

1. Does your brain still work when you are sleeping?
   ● yes   ○ no

2. Is he using his brain to read?
   ● yes   ○ no

3. Is he using his brain to run?
   ● yes   ○ no

4. Can you see the boy's brain?
   ○ yes   ● no

Page 43

The Brain and Skull

Match the word with the picture.

1. brain
2. skull
3. protect

Finish the sentence to tell how your brain helps you.
Then draw a picture about the sentence.

Answers will vary.

My _____ helps me

Page 44

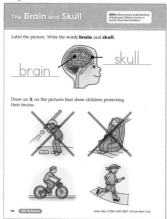

The Brain and Skull

Label the picture. Write the words **brain** and **skull**.

brain   skull

Draw an **X** on the pictures that show children protecting their brains.

Parts of an Insect

Page 50

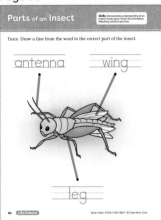

Parts of an Insect — Skills: Demonstrate understanding of an insect's body parts; Visual discrimination; Matching words to pictures

Trace. Draw a line from the word to the correct part of the insect.

antenna   wing

leg

Page 51

Parts of an Insect — Skills: Demonstrate understanding of an insect's body parts; Visual discrimination

Answer the question. Fill in the circle for **yes** or **no**.

1. Does this butterfly have three main body parts? ● yes ○ no
2. Insects have six legs. Is this spider an insect? ○ yes ● no
3. Ants do not have wings. Is this ant an insect? ● yes ○ no
4. Is this bee an insect? ● yes ○ no

Page 52

Parts of an Insect — Skills: Demonstrate understanding of what an insect is; Categorize; Visual discrimination

Color only the insects.

Sample of a completed My Own Insect STEM Challenge

What Do Animals Eat?

Page 58

What Do Animals Eat? — Skills: Demonstrate understanding of carnivores, herbivores, and omnivores; Visual discrimination

Answer the question. Fill in the circle for **yes** or **no**.

1. Does a dog have sharp teeth? ● yes ○ no
2. Do a dog and a pony eat the same food? ○ yes ● no
3. Is this pony a herbivore? ● yes ○ no
4. Is this boy an omnivore? ○ yes ○ no

Page 59

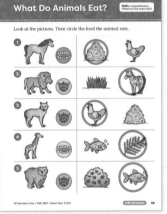

What Do Animals Eat? — Skills: Comprehension; Inference; Fine motor skills

Look at the pictures. Then circle the food the animal eats.

Page 60

What Do Animals Eat? — Skills: Letter formation; Comprehension

Trace the word to complete the sentence. Then read the sentence.

1. A cat eats meat.
2. A deer eats plants.
3. A wolf eats meat.
4. A cow eats plants.

Sample of a completed Wild Thing STEM Challenge

Where Animals Live

Page 66

Where Animals Live — Skills: Comprehension; Inference; Letter formation

Read. Look at the pictures. Circle the correct answer.

1. Which animal lives in the desert?
2. Which plant gives an elf owl shelter in the desert?
3. What is the weather usually like during the day in the desert?

Trace the words. Then read the sentence.

A desert is a habitat.

Page 67

Where Animals Live — Skills: Match words to pictures; Identify animal homes; Letter formation

Draw a line from the word to the picture. Then trace the words and read the sentence.

1. hole
2. den
3. nest
4. A forest is a habitat.

Page 68

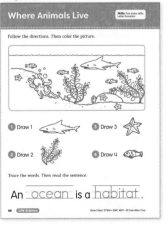

Where Animals Live — Skills: Fine motor skills; Letter formation

Follow the directions. Then color the picture.

1. Draw 1
2. Draw 2
3. Draw 3
4. Draw 4

Trace the words. Then read the sentence.

An ocean is a habitat.

Sample of a completed A Bird's Nest STEM Challenge

Animals in Winter

Page 74

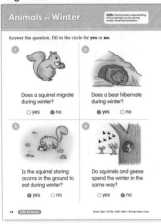

Page 75

Page 76

Sample of a completed
Bear Cave STEM Challenge

Animals and Their Babies

Page 82

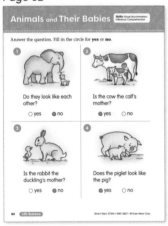

Page 83

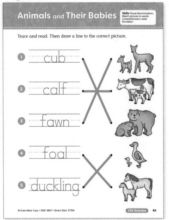

Page 84

Sample of a completed
Pigpen STEM Challenge

The Moon

Page 90

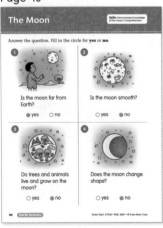

Page 91

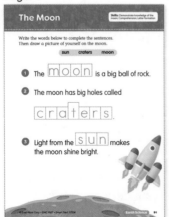

Page 92

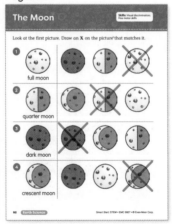

Sample of a completed
Over the Moon
STEM Challenge

Recording the Weather

Page 98

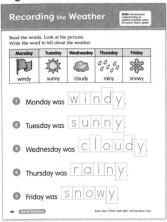

Recording the Weather — Skills: Demonstrate understanding of weather symbols; Letter formation; Read a graph

Read the words. Look at the pictures.
Write the word to tell about the weather.

Monday	Tuesday	Wednesday	Thursday	Friday
windy	sunny	cloudy	rainy	snowy

1. Monday was **windy**.
2. Tuesday was **sunny**.
3. Wednesday was **cloudy**.
4. Thursday was **rainy**.
5. Friday was **snowy**.

Page 99

Recording the Weather — Skills: Demonstrate understanding of weather symbols; Inference; Fine motor skills

Draw a weather symbol in the boxes to tell about the weather.

Page 100

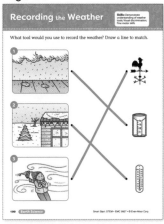

Recording the Weather — Skills: Demonstrate understanding of weather tools; Visual discrimination; Fine motor skills

What tool would you use to record the weather? Draw a line to match.

Bodies of Water

Page 106

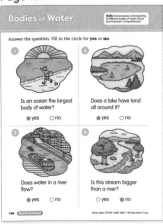

Bodies of Water — Skills: Demonstrate understanding of different bodies of water; Visual discrimination; Comprehension

Answer the question. Fill in the circle for **yes** or **no**.

1. Is an ocean the largest body of water? ● yes ○ no
2. Does a lake have land all around it? ● yes ○ no
3. Does water in a river flow? ● yes ○ no
4. Is this stream bigger than a river? ○ yes ● no

Page 107

Bodies of Water — Skills: Demonstrate understanding of different bodies of water; Visual discrimination; Comprehension; Match words to pictures

Look at the picture. Then trace the word that tells about the picture.

river   lake   stream   ocean

1. ocean
2. lake
3. river
4. stream

Page 108

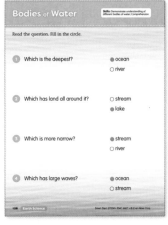

Bodies of Water — Skills: Demonstrate understanding of different bodies of water; Comprehension

Read the question. Fill in the circle.

1. Which is the deepest? ● ocean ○ river
2. Which has land all around it? ○ stream ● lake
3. Which is more narrow? ● stream ○ river
4. Which has large waves? ● ocean ○ stream

Looking at Rocks

Page 114

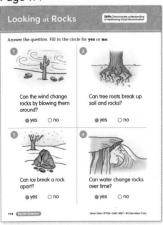

Looking at Rocks — Skills: Demonstrate understanding of weathering; Visual discrimination

Answer the question. Fill in the circle for **yes** or **no**.

1. Can the wind change rocks by blowing them around? ● yes ○ no
2. Can tree roots break up soil and rocks? ● yes ○ no
3. Can ice break a rock apart? ● yes ○ no
4. Can water change rocks over time? ● yes ○ no

Page 115

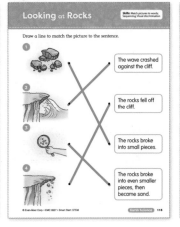

Looking at Rocks — Skills: Match pictures to words; Sequencing; Visual discrimination

Draw a line to match the picture to the sentence.

- The wave crashed against the cliff.
- The rocks fell off the cliff.
- The rocks broke into small pieces.
- The rocks broke into even smaller pieces, then became sand.

Page 116

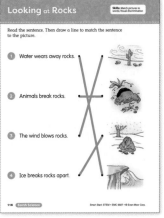

Looking at Rocks — Skills: Match pictures to words; Visual discrimination

Read the sentence. Then draw a line to match the sentence to the picture.

1. Water wears away rocks.
2. Animals break rocks.
3. The wind blows rocks.
4. Ice breaks rocks apart.

Smart Start: STEM • EMC 9927 • © Evan-Moor Corp.